# The MISEDUCATION of the Negro in the 21st Century

High School Teacher's Edition by Cedric A. Washington

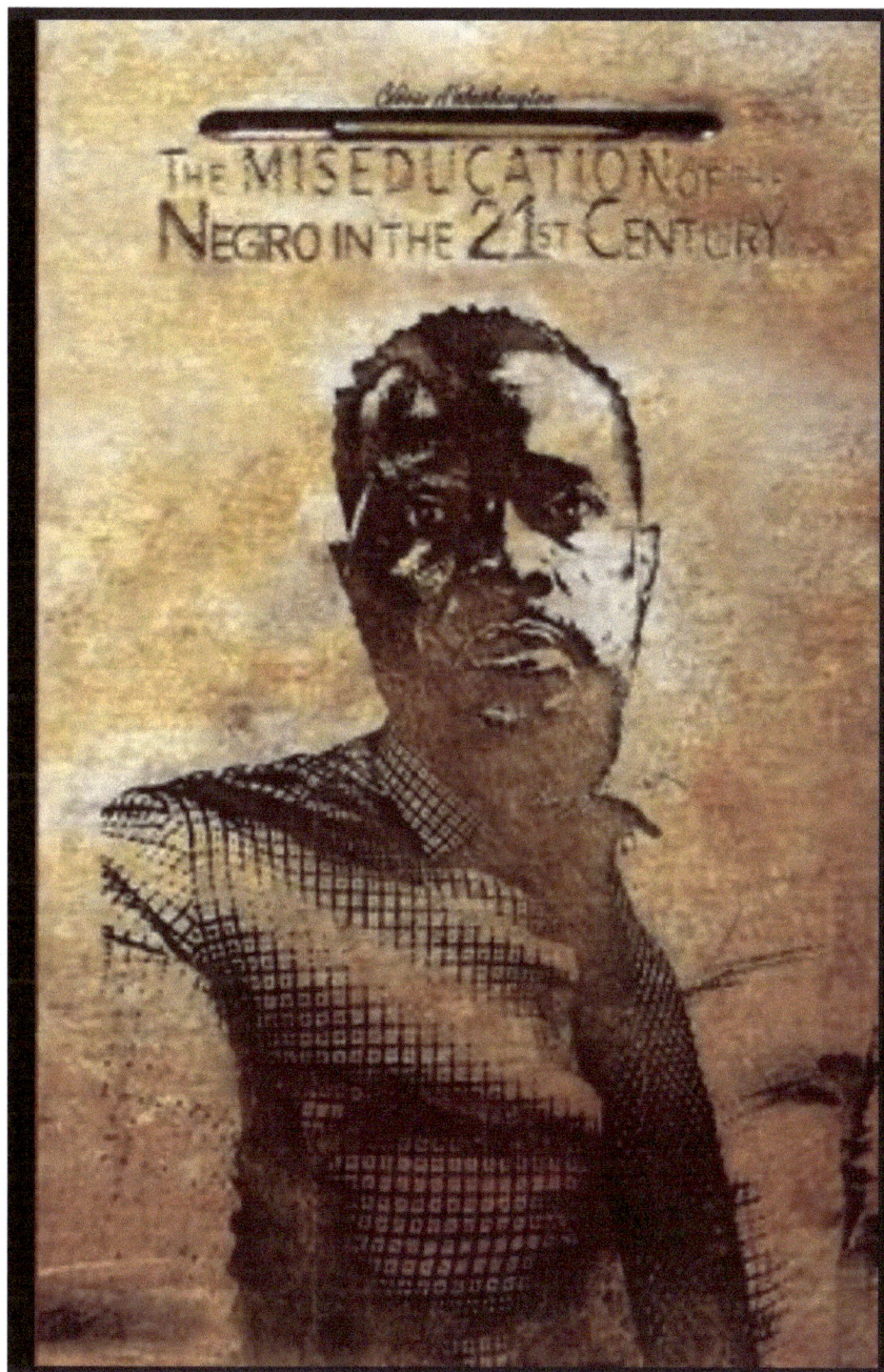

# Dedication

This work is dedicated to every young mind determined to break free from the chains of miseducation. To the students who question, the teachers who empower, and the ancestors whose sacrifices paved the road we walk today.

May this guide serve as a light, a weapon, and a foundation.
Never forget — you were born to lead, not follow.
The world is your classroom. The truth is your legacy.

- Cedric A. Washington
Author. Educator. Revolutionary.

The MISEDUCATION of the Negro in the 21st Century – High School Teacher's Edition
All rights reserved.

Who Lives Like This?! Publishing LLC
www.nerdyouthservices.org

ISBN: 978-1-970680-03-4 (Hardcover)

Cover design and interior layout by
Who Lives Like This?! Publishing LLC Design Team

Printed in the United States of America

First Edition — 2025

# THE MISEDUCATION OF THE NEGRO IN THE 21ST CENTURY

## HIGH SCHOOL TEACHER'S EDITION (GRADES 9–12)

### PREFACE

**Teach Like Ced Series**
**Knowledge of S.E.L.F. (Social Empowerment Learning Framework)**
By **Cedric A. Washington**

---

## TEACHER ORIENTATION (HS LEVEL)

### Instructional Stance

At the high school level, the Preface is treated as a **foundational informational text** that introduces:

- systemic critique
- author positionality
- argument framing
- lived experience as evidence
- education vs. knowledge

Students are expected to **analyze**, **interrogate**, and **synthesize** the author's claims using **textual evidence**, not personal opinion.

---

## CENTRAL CLAIM (FROM THE TEXT)

The academic system known as education suppresses culturally competent pedagogy, forces compliance over humanity, and perpetuates miseducation—particularly in urban schools—while positioning models, data, and standards above lived expertise and truth.

---

# AUTHOR'S PURPOSE (TEXT-BASED)

The author:

- establishes his credibility through lived experience
- exposes systemic contradictions in education
- defines miseducation as a form of control
- introduces **Knowledge vs. Education** as the central tension of the book
- positions **Knowledge of S.E.L.F.** as a corrective framework

---

# STANDARDS ALIGNMENT (HS)

## ELA (Grades 9–12)

- Analyze how an author develops and refines a central argument
- Evaluate the role of anecdotal evidence in informational text
- Determine meanings of words and phrases as used in a text
- Write arguments supported by precise textual evidence
- Participate in academic discussion using accountable talk

## Social Studies

- Examine systems of power and institutional control
- Analyze education as a social institution
- Evaluate historical continuity in oppression and resistance
- Assess identity, culture, and governance

---

# PREFACE — CLOSE READING SECTIONS

## SECTION A — SYSTEMIC EDUCATION

**Key Focus (Teacher):**

- pedagogy vs. standards
- mainstream curriculum
- cultural competency

**Text Anchor:**

"The academic system known as education can stifle the pedagogy of the best teachers..."

## SECTION B — LIVED EXPERIENCE AS EVIDENCE

**Key Focus:**

- institutional discipline
- data-driven models
- compliance vs. correction

**Text Anchor:**

"Redirect, student correct behavior, keep it moving."

---

## SECTION C — MODELS VS. EXPERTISE

**Key Focus:**

- authority
- professional judgment
- misjudgment through compliance

**Text Anchor:**

"Schools pride themselves on a model versus listening to the expert, me."

---

## SECTION D — MIS-EDUCATION AS CONTROL

**Key Focus:**

- pop-up shop schools
- financial pressure
- systemic perpetuation

**Text Anchor:**

"We put out products that we know are not real."

---

## SECTION E — KNOWLEDGE VS. EDUCATION

**Key Focus:**

- definition analysis
- slavery as metaphor and system

**Text Anchor:**

"Can you be educated and still be clueless? That is called slavery."

# VOCABULARY (TEXT-DERIVED — HS LEVEL)

Students analyze **precision of language**, **connotation**, and **systemic meaning**.

| Term | Contextual Meaning (from Preface) |
| --- | --- |
| pedagogy | method of teaching |
| ramifications | consequences of policy |
| mainstream | dominant educational narrative |
| cultural competency | ability to teach within culture |
| institutionalized | conditioned by systems |
| constraints | imposed limitations |
| compliant | obedient to policy |
| data driven | controlled by metrics |
| redirect | correction without punishment |
| insubordinate | perceived defiance |
| pop-up shop schools | temporary, profit-driven institutions |
| perpetuate | continue harm |
| shackles | metaphor for control |
| intellectual jargon | empty academic language |
| biased | structurally unfair |
| destiny | collective future |
| miseducation | harmful education |
| knowledge | lived, applied understanding |
| slavery | control against conscience |
| culture | foundation of intelligence |

# TEXT-DEPENDENT QUESTIONS

## Analytical (Required Evidence)

1. How does the author argue that state standards limit authentic teaching?
2. Why does the author reject data-driven discipline models?
3. How does the shirt-tucking anecdote function as evidence?
4. What does the author mean by "models versus listening to the expert"?
5. How does the author redefine slavery in educational terms?
6. Why does the author position Knowledge of S.E.L.F. as necessary?

---

# IDEAL RESPONSE GUIDANCE (TE ONLY)

- Students must cite **specific moments** from the Preface
- Responses should identify **systems**, not individuals
- Emphasis on **author's reasoning**, not agreement

---

# WRITING TASKS

## Argumentative Constructed Response

**Prompt:**
Analyze how Cedric A. Washington uses personal experience to critique systemic education. Support your response with evidence from the Preface.

---

## Extended Analytical Writing

**Prompt:**
The author claims miseducation is a form of control. Write a multi-paragraph response evaluating this claim using only the Preface.

---

# DISCUSSION FRAME

**Essential Question:**

"Who decides what knowledge is valued in schools?"

**Rules:**

- Cite text
- Challenge ideas, not people
- Academic tone required

---

# KNOWLEDGE OF S.E.L.F. ALIGNMENT — PREFACE

| Domain | Connection |
|---|---|
| SELF Conscience | Awareness of systemic control |
| SELF Governing | Rejecting forced compliance |
| Social Conscience | Collective responsibility |
| Aspirations | Destiny beyond miseducation |

---

# ASSESSMENT RUBRIC (HS — PREFACE)

| Category | Points |
|---|---|
| Textual Evidence | 10 |
| Argument Depth | 10 |
| Vocabulary Precision | 5 |
| Critical Analysis | 5 |
| **Total** | **30** |

# THE MISEDUCATION OF THE NEGRO IN THE 21ST CENTURY

## HIGH SCHOOL TEACHER'S EDITION (GRADES 9–12)

### CHAPTER 1 — PRIVILEGE

**Teach Like Ced Series**
**Knowledge of S.E.L.F. (Social Empowerment Learning Framework)**
By **Cedric A. Washington**

---

## TEACHER ORIENTATION — CHAPTER 1 (HS)

**Instructional Purpose**

At the high school level, **Privilege** is treated as an **argumentative informational text** examining:

- historical continuity of miseducation
- structural privilege
- education as a controlled system
- psychological enslavement
- identity disruption

Students are expected to **analyze claims**, **evaluate historical references**, and **trace cause-and-effect** across time using **textual evidence only**.

---

## CENTRAL CLAIM (TEXT-ANCHORED)

Privilege in America is embedded in education, history, policy, and identity, creating two educational realities—one that develops leadership and innovation, and one that perpetuates psychological enslavement and miseducation.

---

## AUTHOR'S PURPOSE (FROM THE TEXT)

The author:

- exposes how privilege operates systemically
- challenges mainstream education's authority
- situates miseducation as intentional
- calls educators—especially white liberal teachers—to accountability
- frames knowledge of self as essential to liberation

---

# STANDARDS ALIGNMENT (HS)

## ELA (9–12)

- Analyze how an author develops a complex argument
- Evaluate historical and philosophical references
- Determine word meaning through context
- Write analytical arguments grounded in evidence
- Engage in structured academic discourse

## Social Studies

- Examine systemic oppression
- Analyze post-slavery educational structures
- Evaluate historical ideology and propaganda
- Understand identity erasure and power

---

# CHAPTER 1 — TEXT SEGMENTATION (NO EDITS)

## SECTION A — HISTORICAL DEFICIT

- 1980s–2000s
- Charter schools
- Educational disproportionality

**Anchor Line:**

"There has been a deficit of learning in black America..."

---

## SECTION B — WOODSON CONNECTION

- Miseducation as transformation, not development
- Enthusiasm without understanding

**Anchor Line:**

"Their aim was to transform the Negroes, not to develop them."

---

## SECTION C — PRIVILEGE DEFINED

- Constitutional access
- Liberty and justice for all
- Enslavement and delayed freedom

**Anchor Line:**

"To be white in America, one is automatically privy…"

---

## SECTION D — PSYCHOLOGICAL ENSLAVEMENT

- Juneteenth
- Lack of resources
- Identity confusion

---

## SECTION E — PROPAGANDA & SYSTEMS

- Superiority vs. inferiority
- Housing segregation
- Wealth disparities

---

## SECTION F — CALL TO EDUCATORS

- White liberal teachers
- Advocacy
- African American Studies

---

# VOCABULARY (TEXT-DERIVED — HS LEVEL)

Students examine **historical, political, and psychological weight** of words.

| Term | Meaning from Context |
|---|---|
| deficit | absence of learning |
| disproportionality | unequal distribution |
| plague | widespread harm |
| charter schools | pop-up institutions |
| mainstream | dominant narrative |
| rhetoric | empty language |
| privilege | systemic access |
| psychologically enslaved | mentally controlled |
| propaganda | ideological conditioning |
| superiority | imposed hierarchy |
| inferiority | imposed deficiency |
| systematic structure | organized control |
| dissipated | erased |
| knowledge of self | identity awareness |
| advocate | speak against injustice |
| ally | supportive but responsible |
| independence | self-determination |

# TEXT-DEPENDENT QUESTIONS (HS)

## Analytical — Evidence Required

1. How does the author trace educational deficit across decades?
2. Why does the author criticize charter schools specifically?
3. How does Carter G. Woodson's quote support the author's argument?
4. What does privilege mean beyond wealth in this chapter?
5. How does psychological enslavement continue after Juneteenth?
6. Why does the author argue African American Studies is necessary?

# IDEAL RESPONSE GUIDANCE (TE ONLY)

- Responses must cite **specific historical references**
- Students should identify **systems, not individuals**
- Emphasis on **cause-and-effect reasoning**

# WRITING TASKS (HS)

### Constructed Analytical Response

**Prompt:**
Analyze how privilege operates in education according to Chapter 1. Use textual evidence to support your analysis.

---

### Extended Argument

**Prompt:**
The author argues miseducation is intentional. Write a multi-paragraph argument explaining how privilege sustains miseducation, using only Chapter 1.

---

# DISCUSSION PROTOCOL (HS)

### Essential Question:

"Can education be neutral in a system built on privilege?"

Rules:

- Text citations required
- Respectful challenge
- Academic language only

---

# KNOWLEDGE OF S.E.L.F. ALIGNMENT — CHAPTER 1

| Domain | Text Connection |
|---|---|
| SELF Conscience | Awareness of privilege |
| SELF Governing | Rejecting imposed narratives |
| Social Conscience | Collective responsibility |
| Aspirations | Liberation through knowledge |

---

# ASSESSMENT RUBRIC — HS CHAPTER 1

| Category | Points |
| --- | --- |
| Textual Evidence | 10 |
| Analytical Depth | 10 |
| Vocabulary Precision | 5 |
| Reasoning & Clarity | 5 |
| **Total** | **30** |

# THE MISEDUCATION OF THE NEGRO IN THE 21ST CENTURY

## HIGH SCHOOL TEACHER'S EDITION (GRADES 9–12)

### CHAPTER 2 — FIGUREHEAD

**Teach Like Ced Series**
**Knowledge of S.E.L.F. (Social Empowerment Learning Framework)**
By **Cedric A. Washington**

---

## TEACHER ORIENTATION — CHAPTER 2 (HS)

### Instructional Purpose

At the high school level, **Figurehead** functions as a **critical leadership and systems analysis** chapter. Students examine how **symbolic authority**, **institutional compliance**, and **job security** sustain miseducation even when leadership positions are occupied by Black administrators.

Students are expected to:

- analyze leadership beyond titles
- evaluate power vs. authority
- examine internalized miseducation
- trace institutional accountability

---

## CENTRAL CLAIM (TEXT-ANCHORED)

Figurehead leadership in education creates the illusion of progress while maintaining systems of oppression, particularly when Black principals are positioned to enforce policies that harm Black students rather than challenge them.

---

# AUTHOR'S PURPOSE (FROM THE TEXT)

The author:

- defines figurehead leadership using lived experience and historical reference
- exposes how Black leadership is constrained by white-controlled systems
- connects miseducation to compliance and job security
- challenges Black principals to awaken conscience and reject symbolic power

---

# STANDARDS ALIGNMENT (HS)

## ELA (9–12)

- Analyze complex ideas and power structures in informational texts
- Evaluate historical quotations and their relevance
- Determine meaning of words with political and social weight
- Write analytical arguments with evidence
- Participate in evidence-based discussion

## Social Studies

- Examine leadership in institutional systems
- Analyze power, authority, and governance
- Evaluate the school-to-prison pipeline
- Understand systemic control and internalized oppression

---

# CHAPTER 2 — TEXT SEGMENTATION (NO EDITS)

## SECTION A — FIGUREHEAD-ISMS

- "Play the game"
- "This is how they want it done"

**Anchor Concept:** Nominal leadership

---

## SECTION B — WOODSON & ENSLAVED MINDS

- "Highly educated Negroes"
- Defending the system

---

## SECTION C — BLACK PRINCIPALS & COMPLIANCE

- Badge of honor
- Shaking and nodding
- Job security

---

## SECTION D — DISCIPLINE & CONTROL

- "Sweat the small stuff"
- School-to-prison pipeline
- Zero tolerance

---

## SECTION E — HOUSE NEGRO ANALOGY

- Symbolic authority
- Enforcing oppression

---

## SECTION F — CALL TO CONSCIENCE

- Rejecting figurehead status
- Teaching culture
- Breaking the hamster wheel

---

# VOCABULARY (TEXT-DERIVED — HS LEVEL)

Students examine **political, institutional, and psychological meaning**.

| Term | Meaning from Context |
|---|---|
| figurehead | leader without real power |
| nominal | in name only |
| enslaved mind | controlled thinking |
| compliance | obedience to authority |
| badge of honor | status symbol |
| muzzle | silencing |
| dysfunctionality | perceived disorder |
| exploit | harm for security |
| doctrine | imposed belief system |
| school-to-prison pipeline | policies pushing students toward incarceration |
| tyrannical | oppressive control |
| desegregation | racial integration |
| house negro | enforcer of oppression |
| conscience | moral awareness |
| hamster wheel | endless cycle without progress |

# TEXT-DEPENDENT QUESTIONS (HS)

## Analytical — Evidence Required

1. What are "figurehead-isms," and how do they function in schools?
2. How does Woodson's quote explain internalized miseducation?
3. Why does the author argue Black principals are "between a rock and a hard place"?
4. How does discipline policy connect to the school-to-prison pipeline?
5. Why does the author use the house negro analogy?
6. What does awakening conscience require of Black leadership?

# IDEAL RESPONSE GUIDANCE (TE ONLY)

- Students must distinguish **power vs. position**
- Analysis should focus on **systems**, not individuals
- Responses must cite **specific language from the chapter**

# WRITING TASKS (HS)

## Constructed Analytical Response

**Prompt:**
Analyze how figurehead leadership sustains miseducation in schools. Use evidence from Chapter 2.

## Extended Argument

**Prompt:**
Evaluate the author's claim that symbolic leadership is more harmful than honest absence of leadership. Support your argument using Chapter 2 only.

# DISCUSSION PROTOCOL (HS)

**Essential Question:**

"Is leadership about authority or courage?"

Rules:

- Textual evidence required
- No personal attacks
- Respectful academic debate

# KNOWLEDGE OF S.E.L.F. ALIGNMENT — CHAPTER 2

| Domain | Text Connection |
|---|---|
| SELF Conscience | Moral awakening |
| SELF Governing | Rejecting compliance |
| Social Conscience | Responsibility to community |
| Good People Skills | Ethical leadership |

# ASSESSMENT RUBRIC — HS CHAPTER 2

| Category | Points |
| --- | --- |
| Textual Evidence | 10 |
| Depth of Analysis | 10 |
| Vocabulary Precision | 5 |
| Logical Reasoning | 5 |
| **Total** | **30** |

# THE MISEDUCATION OF THE NEGRO IN THE 21ST CENTURY

## HIGH SCHOOL TEACHER'S EDITION (GRADES 9–12)

### CHAPTER 3 — KNOWLEDGE vs. EDUCATION

**Teach Like Ced Series**
**Knowledge of S.E.L.F. (Social Empowerment Learning Framework)**
By **Cedric A. Washington**

---

## TEACHER ORIENTATION — CHAPTER 3 (HS)

**Instructional Purpose**

At the high school level, **Knowledge vs. Education** functions as a **conceptual and analytical pivot** of the text. Students interrogate:

- definitions as power
- control of information
- identity as prerequisite to self-awareness
- limitations of mainstream SEL
- miseducation as modern slavery

Students are expected to **compare definitions**, **analyze frameworks**, and **evaluate consequences** using **textual evidence only**.

---

## CENTRAL CLAIM (TEXT-ANCHORED)

Education without knowledge creates controlled individuals who lack identity, critical thinking, and wisdom; when an oppressor controls education, miseducation becomes a system of mental enslavement.

---

# AUTHOR'S PURPOSE (FROM THE TEXT)

The author:

- distinguishes **education** from **knowledge** through definition
- critiques mainstream SEL as culturally shallow
- introduces **identity** as essential to self-awareness
- explains **cognitive dissonance** as a barrier to truth
- positions **Knowledge of S.E.L.F.** as corrective and empowering

---

# STANDARDS ALIGNMENT (HS)

## ELA (9–12)

- Analyze how definitions shape argument
- Evaluate frameworks using evidence
- Determine meaning of academic and psychological terms
- Write explanatory and argumentative texts
- Engage in structured academic discussion

## Social Studies

- Examine identity and power
- Analyze systems of control
- Evaluate social-emotional policy impacts
- Understand cultural conditioning

---

# CHAPTER 3 — TEXT SEGMENTATION (NO EDITS)

## SECTION A — DEFINITIONS AS CONTROL

- Knowledge (Oxford Languages)
- Education (Oxford Languages)
- Synonyms vs. distinctions

**Anchor Concept:** Who controls learning

---

## SECTION B — OPPRESSION & MISEDUCATION

- "If your oppressor controls your academic intelligence…"
- Education as system of limitation

---

## SECTION C — SEL & ONE-SIZE-FITS-ALL

- CASEL model
- Five core competencies
- Shallow application

---

## SECTION D — SELF-AWARENESS & IDENTITY

- Identity definition (Merriam-Webster)
- Overgeneralization
- Preconceived notions

---

## SECTION E — COGNITIVE DISSONANCE

- Inconsistent beliefs
- Resistance to truth
- Naming and skin color

---

## SECTION F — KNOWLEDGE OF S.E.L.F.

- Five mastery steps
- Love Yourself (The Skin You're In)
- Empowerment through identity

---

# VOCABULARY (TEXT-DERIVED — HS LEVEL)

Students analyze **precision, implication, and consequence**.

| Term | Meaning from Context |
| --- | --- |
| knowledge | lived and applied understanding |
| education | systematic instruction |
| oppressor | controller of systems |
| miseducation | harmful instruction |
| SEL | behavioral-academic framework |
| self-awareness | understanding internal cues |
| identity | distinguishing character |
| preconceived notion | assumption |
| overgeneralizing | grouping without context |
| cultural characteristics | shared traits |
| cognitive dissonance | conflicting beliefs |
| melanin | skin pigment |
| complexion | skin tone |
| connotation | implied meaning |
| intentional | deliberate |
| wisdom | applied knowledge |

---

# TEXT-DEPENDENT QUESTIONS (HS)

## Analytical — Evidence Required

1. Why does the author begin with dictionary definitions?
2. How does control of education lead to miseducation?
3. Why does the author critique CASEL's self-awareness model?
4. How does identity function as a prerequisite to self-awareness?
5. What role does cognitive dissonance play in resisting truth?
6. How does the "Love Yourself (The Skin You're In)" lesson disrupt miseducation?

---

# IDEAL RESPONSE GUIDANCE (TE ONLY)

- Students must cite **definitions and examples**
- Responses should connect **identity → awareness → empowerment**
- Analysis should remain **text-anchored**

# WRITING TASKS (HS)

## Constructed Analytical Response

**Prompt:**
Explain how the author distinguishes knowledge from education and why this distinction matters. Use evidence from Chapter 3.

## Extended Argument

**Prompt:**
Evaluate the claim that education without knowledge is slavery. Support your argument using only Chapter 3.

# DISCUSSION PROTOCOL (HS)

## Essential Question:

"Can self-awareness exist without identity?"

Rules:

- Textual evidence required
- Academic tone
- Respectful challenge

# KNOWLEDGE OF S.E.L.F. ALIGNMENT — CHAPTER 3

| Domain | Text Connection |
|---|---|
| SELF Conscience | Identity awareness |
| SELF Governing | Independent thought |
| Social Conscience | Empowering others |
| Aspirations | Purpose and growth |

# ASSESSMENT RUBRIC — HS CHAPTER 3

| Category | Points |
|---|---|
| Textual Evidence | 10 |
| Conceptual Depth | 10 |
| Vocabulary Precision | 5 |
| Logical Reasoning | 5 |
| **Total** | **30** |

# THE MISEDUCATION OF THE NEGRO IN THE 21ST CENTURY

## HIGH SCHOOL TEACHER'S EDITION (GRADES 9–12)

### CHAPTER 4 — CULTURE = INTELLIGENCE = BEHAVIOR

**Teach Like Ced Series**
**Knowledge of S.E.L.F. (Social Empowerment Learning Framework)**
By **Cedric A. Washington**

---

## TEACHER ORIENTATION — CHAPTER 4 (HS)

### Instructional Purpose

At the high school level, **Culture = Intelligence = Behavior** is treated as a **theoretical framework chapter** that explains how **environment, conditioning, and historical trauma** shape thinking patterns and actions across generations.

Students are expected to:

- analyze cause-and-effect relationships
- interpret historical theory and modern examples
- evaluate how culture operates as a system
- synthesize ideas across psychology, history, and education

All analysis must be **anchored directly to the chapter text**.

---

## CENTRAL CLAIM (TEXT-ANCHORED)

Culture determines how intelligence is expressed, which in turn shapes behavior; when culture is distorted through miseducation and historical manipulation, behavior reflects that distortion rather than inherent ability.

---

# AUTHOR'S PURPOSE (FROM THE TEXT)

# STANDARDS ALIGNMENT (HS)

## ELA (9–12)

- Analyze development of complex ideas across a text
- Determine meaning of discipline-specific vocabulary
- Analyze analogies, examples, and cultural references
- Write explanatory and argumentative texts using evidence

## Social Studies

- Examine historical conditioning and social control
- Analyze continuity of oppression
- Evaluate how environment shapes identity and behavior
- Interpret historical theory in modern context

---

# CHAPTER 4 — TEXT SEGMENTATION (NO EDITS)

## SECTION A — THE FRAMEWORK

- Culture
- Intelligence
- Behavior

**Anchor Concept:** Sequential relationship

---

## SECTION B — HISTORICAL BASE

- Substantial original historical base
- Correct and re-correct the mind
- Phenomenon vs. illusion

---

## SECTION C — WILLIE LYNCH THEORY

- Conditioning
- Division
- Long-term behavioral impact

---

## SECTION D — MODERN MANIFESTATIONS

- Disproportionality
- Insecurities
- Standards of beauty
- Neutralization

---

## SECTION E — FILM & ANALOGY

- *Trading Places*
- Environmental shift experiment

---

## SECTION F — RECLAMATION

- Exposure to truth
- Cultural reconnection
- Conscious correction

---

# VOCABULARY (TEXT-DERIVED — HS LEVEL)

Students examine **conceptual precision and implication**.

| Term | Meaning from Context |
|------|---------------------|
| phenomenon | observable occurrence |
| correct and re-correct | mental adjustment through truth |
| historical base | foundational truth |
| illusion | false perception |
| orbit | cycle of influence |
| bourgeoisies | ruling class |
| authenticity | genuine expression |
| audacity | boldness |
| rearing | upbringing |
| idiosyncrasies | learned behaviors |
| paranoia | conditioned fear |
| disproportionality | unequal outcomes |
| insecurities | internalized doubt |
| standard of beauty | imposed ideal |
| neutralized | stripped of power |
| product of your environment | conditioned outcome |

---

# TEXT-DEPENDENT QUESTIONS (HS)

## Analytical — Evidence Required

1. Why does the author connect culture directly to intelligence?
2. How does historical conditioning influence present-day behavior?
3. What does "correct and re-correct the mind" mean in the chapter?
4. How does Willie Lynch theory support the framework?
5. Why does the author reference *Trading Places*?
6. How does reconnecting to origin disrupt miseducation?

---

# IDEAL RESPONSE GUIDANCE (TE ONLY)

- Students must trace **culture → intelligence → behavior**
- Analysis should emphasize **conditioning, not deficiency**
- Responses must reference **historical and modern examples**

# WRITING TASKS (HS)

## Constructed Analytical Response

**Prompt:**
Explain how the author proves that behavior is learned rather than innate. Use evidence from Chapter 4.

## Extended Explanatory Writing

**Prompt:**
Write a multi-paragraph explanation analyzing how distorted culture leads to distorted intelligence and behavior, using only Chapter 4.

# DISCUSSION PROTOCOL (HS)

## Essential Question:

"Is behavior a choice or a condition?"

Rules:

- Cite the text
- Academic language required
- Respectful challenge

# KNOWLEDGE OF S.E.L.F. ALIGNMENT — CHAPTER 4

| Domain | Text Connection |
| --- | --- |
| SELF Conscience | Cultural awareness |
| SELF Governing | Reclaiming identity |
| Social Conscience | Collective healing |
| Aspirations | Conscious evolution |

# ASSESSMENT RUBRIC — HS CHAPTER 4

| Category | Points |
|---|---|
| Textual Evidence | 10 |
| Conceptual Analysis | 10 |
| Vocabulary Precision | 5 |
| Logical Organization | 5 |
| **Total** | **30** |

# THE MISEDUCATION OF THE NEGRO IN THE 21ST CENTURY

## HIGH SCHOOL TEACHER'S EDITION (GRADES 9–12)

### CHAPTER 5 — PARENTS AND THE ENVIRONMENT

**Knowledge of S.E.L.F. (Social Empowerment Learning Framework)**
By **Cedric A. Washington**

---

## TEACHER ORIENTATION — CHAPTER 5 (HS)

**Instructional Focus**

Chapter 5 expands the **Culture = Intelligence = Behavior** framework by examining **parental influence, community norms, and environmental conditioning** as mechanisms that perpetuate miseducation across generations.

At the high school level, students are expected to:

- analyze generational transmission of behavior
- examine environmental accountability
- interpret trauma as inherited conditioning
- distinguish responsibility from blame

---

## CENTRAL CLAIM (TEXT-ANCHORED)

When parents and environments are shaped by miseducation, they unintentionally transmit misinformed intelligence, resulting in repeated cycles of behavior that sustain community dysfunction.

---

## AUTHOR'S PURPOSE (FROM THE TEXT)

The author:

- connects historical trauma to modern parenting practices

- explains how environment molds intelligence
- challenges parents to reclaim accountability
- identifies the community as a collective teacher
- exposes the illusion of behavioral surprise

---

# CHAPTER STRUCTURE (NO EDITS)

## SECTION A — KNOWING VS. NOT KNOWING

- "When you know better, you do better"
- Questioning whether knowing ever occurred

---

## SECTION B — WILLIE LYNCH REVISITED

- Destruction of the black male
- Psychological fear conditioning
- Gendered manipulation

---

## SECTION C — THE ABSENT MALE

- Disproportionate household leadership
- Loss of protector/provider role
- Community imbalance

---

## SECTION D — MISINFORMED PARENTS

- Passive participation in schooling
- Acceptance of school authority
- Behavioral normalization

---

## SECTION E — COMMUNITY COLLAPSE

- Loss of collective accountability
- Breakdown of communal correction
- Shift from village to isolation

## SECTION F — STUDENT BEHAVIOR

- Resistance to intelligence
- Fear of appearing smart
- Defense mechanisms

## SECTION G — CALL TO OWNERSHIP

- Parents reclaiming responsibility
- Environment control
- Collective organization

# VOCABULARY (TEXT-DERIVED — HS)

Students analyze **cause-based terminology**.

| Term | Contextual Meaning |
| --- | --- |
| absenteeism | absence from responsibility |
| disproportion | unequal presence |
| protector | guardian role |
| provider | sustainer role |
| accountability | ownership of outcomes |
| misinformed | lacking accurate knowledge |
| vulgarity | degraded communication |
| disrespect | normalized behavior |
| pipeline | systematic progression |
| intervention | corrective action |
| environment | conditioned space |
| collective | shared responsibility |
| normalcy | accepted dysfunction |
| defense mechanism | protective behavior |
| disillusion | false belief |

# TEXT-DEPENDENT QUESTIONS (HS)

## Analytical (Evidence Required)

1. Why does the author question the phrase "when you know better, you do better"?
2. How does the Willie Lynch theory reappear in modern parenting?
3. What role does the absence of the black male play in community outcomes?
4. Why are parents often not surprised by student behavior?
5. How does the environment function as a teacher?
6. Why do students resist appearing intelligent?

---

# IDEAL RESPONSE GUIDANCE (TE ONLY)

Responses should:

- trace behavior back to environment and parenting
- avoid blaming individuals
- emphasize conditioning and repetition
- reference generational transmission

---

# WRITING TASKS (HS)

## Explanatory Essay

**Prompt:**
Explain how misinformed parents and unhealthy environments contribute to the continuation of miseducation, using evidence from Chapter 5.

---

## Argumentative Writing

**Prompt:**
Argue whether responsibility for change begins with parents, schools, or the community. Support your position using Chapter 5 only.

---

# DISCUSSION PROTOCOL (HS)

**Essential Question:**

"Who teaches children when parents and schools fail?"

Guidelines:

- Cite specific sections
- Challenge ideas, not people
- Maintain academic tone

# KNOWLEDGE OF S.E.L.F. ALIGNMENT — CHAPTER 5

| Domain | Text Connection |
|---|---|
| SELF Conscience | Parental awareness |
| SELF Governing | Behavioral correction |
| Social Conscience | Community responsibility |
| Aspirations | Environmental improvement |

# ASSESSMENT RUBRIC — HS CHAPTER 5

| Category | Points |
|---|---|
| Textual Accuracy | 10 |
| Depth of Analysis | 10 |
| Vocabulary Precision | 5 |
| Logical Reasoning | 5 |
| **Total** | **30** |

# THE MISEDUCATION OF THE NEGRO IN THE 21ST CENTURY

## HIGH SCHOOL TEACHER'S EDITION (GRADES 9–12)

### CHAPTER 6 — HIP-HOP

**Knowledge of S.E.L.F. (Social Empowerment Learning Framework)**
By **Cedric A. Washington**

---

## TEACHER ORIENTATION — CHAPTER 6 (HS)

**Instructional Focus**

Chapter 6 positions **Hip-Hop as culture, communicator, and conditioner**. At the high school level, students critically examine how **art influences intelligence and behavior**, and how **economic control of culture mirrors historical systems of domination**.

This chapter requires:

- media literacy
- historical comparison
- ethical reasoning
- cultural accountability

---

## CENTRAL CLAIM (TEXT-ANCHORED)

Hip-Hop, as a dominant cultural force, has the power either to inform, empower, and liberate, or to miseducate, condition, and perpetuate destructive behavior depending on who controls the narrative and intent.

---

## AUTHOR'S PURPOSE (FROM THE TEXT)

The author:

- traces Hip-Hop's origins as cultural expression

- exposes exploitation within the music industry
- connects artistic output to behavioral outcomes
- challenges artists' responsibility to the people
- reclaims Hip-Hop as a teaching tool, not a product

---

# CHAPTER STRUCTURE (TEXT-FAITHFUL)

## SECTION A — CULTURAL ORIGINS

- Creation in inner cities
- Expression of struggle
- Global expansion

---

## SECTION B — INDUSTRY STRUCTURE

- "Master" and "slave" terminology
- Intellectual property control
- Financial exploitation

---

## SECTION C — HOUSE NEGRO VS. FIELD NEGRO

- Privilege vs. masses
- Selling the image
- Division within culture

---

## SECTION D — MUSIC AS CONDITIONING

- Mood setting
- Behavioral influence
- Desensitization

---

## SECTION E — LANGUAGE & IDENTITY

- Normalization of "nigger/nigga"
- Cognitive dissonance

- Misidentification

---

## SECTION F — CULTURAL RESPONSIBILITY

- Artists' conscience
- Teaching vs. selling
- Narrative control

---

# VOCABULARY (TEXT-DERIVED — HS)

Students analyze **cultural-economic language**.

| Term | Meaning from Text |
| --- | --- |
| genre | cultural category |
| exploitation | unfair use |
| intellectual property | creative ownership |
| master | original recording |
| slave | reproduced copy |
| confidant | trusted insider |
| privilege | sanctioned advantage |
| emulate | imitate |
| bravado | exaggerated confidence |
| machismo | aggressive masculinity |
| desensitized | emotionally dulled |
| cognitive dissonance | conflicting beliefs |
| connotation | implied meaning |
| narrative | controlled story |
| conscience | moral awareness |

---

# TEXT-DEPENDENT QUESTIONS (HS)

## Critical Analysis

1. Why does the author describe Hip-Hop as "the black CNN"?
2. How does the music industry structure resemble slavery?
3. What is the significance of "master" and "slave" terminology?

4. How does Hip-Hop influence behavior beyond entertainment?
5. Why does the author connect rappers to the house negro analogy?
6. How does language usage contribute to miseducation?
7. What responsibility does Hip-Hop have to the culture?

# IDEAL RESPONSE GUIDANCE (TE ONLY)

Students should:

- distinguish between **expression vs. exploitation**
- explain how **culture teaches behavior**
- recognize **economic control of narratives**
- avoid moral absolutism; analyze responsibility

# WRITING TASKS (HS)

## Analytical Essay

**Prompt:**
Analyze how Hip-Hop functions as both a tool of empowerment and a mechanism of miseducation in Chapter 6.

## Argumentative Writing

**Prompt:**
Should Hip-Hop artists be held accountable for the behavior their music influences? Use evidence from the text.

# DISCUSSION PROTOCOL (HS)

## Essential Question:

"Does art imitate life, or does life imitate art?"

Rules:

- Cite specific examples from the chapter
- Respect lived experiences
- Maintain academic discourse

# KNOWLEDGE OF S.E.L.F. ALIGNMENT — CHAPTER 6

| Domain | Text Connection |
|---|---|
| SELF Conscience | Cultural awareness |
| SELF Governing | Language accountability |
| Social Conscience | Collective responsibility |
| Aspirations | Cultural preservation |

# ASSESSMENT RUBRIC — HS CHAPTER 6

| Category | Points |
|---|---|
| Textual Accuracy | 10 |
| Cultural Analysis | 10 |
| Vocabulary Precision | 5 |
| Critical Reasoning | 5 |
| **Total** | **30** |

# THE MISEDUCATION OF THE NEGRO IN THE 21ST CENTURY

## HIGH SCHOOL TEACHER'S EDITION (GRADES 9–12)

### CHAPTER 7 — POLITICS

**Knowledge of S.E.L.F. (Social Empowerment Learning Framework)**
By **Cedric A. Washington**

---

## TEACHER ORIENTATION — CHAPTER 7 (HS)

**Instructional Focus**

Chapter 7 examines **political identity, participation, and disillusionment** as products of miseducation. At the high school level, this chapter supports **civic literacy**, **historical awareness**, and **critical evaluation of political allegiance** without partisan instruction.

Students are guided to:

- analyze historical timelines and contradictions
- evaluate political participation vs. outcomes
- examine identity-based voting behavior
- distinguish symbolism from structural change

---

## CENTRAL CLAIM (TEXT-ANCHORED)

Despite sustained political participation and loyalty, the so-called African American community continues to experience unmet demands for opportunities, employment, and justice, revealing political miseducation rather than political empowerment.

---

# AUTHOR'S PURPOSE (FROM THE TEXT)

The author:

- traces Black political participation historically
- exposes contradictions between promises and outcomes
- challenges blind allegiance to political parties
- reframes political power as collective organization
- urges self-determined agendas over partisan dependency

---

# CHAPTER STRUCTURE (TEXT-FAITHFUL)

## SECTION A — SYMBOLIC LANGUAGE

- The Pledge of Allegiance
- "Liberty and justice for all"
- National contradictions

---

## SECTION B — HISTORICAL TIMELINE

- Slavery
- Jim Crow
- Civil Rights
- Voting Rights Act

---

## SECTION C — PARTY POLITICS

- Republican vs. Democrat roles
- Presidential milestones
- Repeated outcomes

---

## SECTION D — HIP-HOP & POLITICAL MOBILIZATION

- "Vote or Die"
- Cultural influence
- Voter turnout

## SECTION E — CONTINUED DISPARITY

- Opportunities
- Employment
- Justice

## SECTION F — ECONOMIC POWER

- Black dollar
- Collective spending
- Community ownership

## SECTION G — COLLECTIVE RESPONSIBILITY

- Black agenda
- Organization
- Self-sufficiency

# VOCABULARY (TEXT-DERIVED — HS)

Students examine **political language and implication**.

| Term | Contextual Meaning |
|------|--------------------|
| allegiance | loyalty |
| democracy | voting system |
| rhetoric | persuasive language |
| disproportionality | unequal outcomes |
| agenda | collective priorities |
| allegiance politics | party loyalty |
| symbolism | representational gestures |
| mobilization | organized participation |
| patronize | financially support |
| collective | unified group |
| hamster wheel | repetitive cycle |
| glass ceiling | invisible limitation |

| Term | Contextual Meaning |
|---|---|
| classism | social stratification |
| economic power | financial influence |

# TEXT-DEPENDENT QUESTIONS (HS)

## Civic Analysis

1. Why does the author emphasize the wording of the Pledge of Allegiance?
2. How does history challenge the promise of "liberty and justice for all"?
3. Why does the author critique both political parties?
4. How did Hip-Hop influence voter mobilization?
5. Why does political representation not equate to political empowerment?
6. What does the author identify as the true source of power?

# IDEAL RESPONSE GUIDANCE (TE ONLY)

Students should:

- reference historical sequences
- distinguish participation from results
- analyze power beyond voting
- avoid partisan bias

# WRITING TASKS (HS)

## Explanatory Essay

**Prompt:**
Explain why the author argues that political participation has not resulted in political empowerment for Black Americans.

## Argumentative Writing

**Prompt:**
Should Black communities rely on political parties or build independent agendas? Support your argument using Chapter 7 only.

# DISCUSSION PROTOCOL (HS)

**Essential Question:**

"Is voting power without economic power effective?"

Discussion norms:

- Cite text
- No party advocacy
- Focus on systems

# KNOWLEDGE OF S.E.L.F. ALIGNMENT — CHAPTER 7

| Domain | Text Connection |
|---|---|
| SELF Conscience | Political awareness |
| SELF Governing | Independent decision-making |
| Social Conscience | Collective action |
| Aspirations | Economic self-determination |

# ASSESSMENT RUBRIC — HS CHAPTER 7

| Category | Points |
|---|---|
| Historical Accuracy | 10 |
| Analytical Depth | 10 |
| Vocabulary Precision | 5 |
| Civic Reasoning | 5 |
| **Total** | **30** |

# THE MISEDUCATION OF THE NEGRO IN THE 21ST CENTURY

## HIGH SCHOOL TEACHER'S EDITION (GRADES 9–12)

### CHAPTER 8 — THE BLACK CHURCH

**Knowledge of S.E.L.F. (Social Empowerment Learning Framework)**
By **Cedric A. Washington**

---

## TEACHER ORIENTATION — CHAPTER 8 (HS)

**Instructional Focus**

Chapter 8 interrogates **religion as a system of control, conditioning, and miseducation** while simultaneously acknowledging its historical role in Black survival and resistance. At the high school level, this chapter requires **mature facilitation**, **text fidelity**, and **clear boundaries between analysis and belief**.

Students are expected to:

- analyze religion as a historical institution
- distinguish faith from manipulation
- evaluate cognitive dissonance within belief systems
- understand separation of church and state as structural, not spiritual

---

## CENTRAL CLAIM (TEXT-ANCHORED)

The Black Church, while historically central to Black life, has become one of the most powerful instruments of miseducation by prioritizing spiritual consolation over collective liberation, thereby sustaining confusion, dependency, and inaction.

---

# AUTHOR'S PURPOSE (FROM THE TEXT)

The author:

- exposes how Christianity was used to control enslaved people
- critiques modern church disengagement from political and social realities
- examines cognitive dissonance in religious belief
- highlights contradictions between scripture, history, and lived experience
- calls for revelation and reclaimed understanding

---

# CHAPTER STRUCTURE (TEXT-FAITHFUL)

## SECTION A — CONTROL OF THE MIND

- "Keep the body and destroy the mind"
- Psychological conditioning
- Cognitive dissonance

---

## SECTION B — RELIGION AS MANIPULATION

- Shared religion of oppressor and oppressed
- Slave preachers
- Selective scripture

---

## SECTION C — SEPARATION OF CHURCH AND STATE

- 501(c)(3) restrictions
- Political silence
- Institutional fear

---

## SECTION D — HISTORICAL CONTRADICTIONS

- Nat Turner
- Dr. Martin Luther King Jr.
- Malcolm X
- Elijah Muhammad

## SECTION E — MODERN BLACK CHURCH

- Entertainment-based worship
- Individual prosperity
- Fragmentation

## SECTION F — LOSS OF COLLECTIVE DIRECTION

- Multiple agendas
- Lack of unity
- Waiting instead of building

## SECTION G — REVELATION

- Identity
- Origin
- Truth recognition

# VOCABULARY (TEXT-DERIVED — HS)

Students examine **theological and sociopolitical language**.

| Term | Meaning from Context |
|------|----------------------|
| manipulation | deceptive control |
| cognitive dissonance | conflicting belief |
| denomination | religious division |
| interpretation | assigned meaning |
| oppression | systemic domination |
| separation | institutional division |
| 501(c)(3) | tax-exempt restriction |
| prosperity | material success |
| illusion | false belief |
| doctrine | religious teaching |
| revelation | disclosed truth |
| congregation | gathered believers |

| Term | Meaning from Context |
|------|---------------------|
| silence | institutional restraint |
| neutrality | avoidance of stance |
| worship | religious devotion |

# TEXT-DEPENDENT QUESTIONS (HS)

## Critical Theology & Society Analysis

1. How was Christianity used as a tool of control during slavery?
2. Why does the author criticize the Black Church's political silence?
3. How does cognitive dissonance appear in modern religious belief?
4. What contradictions does the author highlight regarding Jesus?
5. Why were Nat Turner, Dr. King, and Malcolm X met with resistance?
6. How has the Black Church shifted from collective liberation to individual prosperity?
7. What does the author mean by revelation?

# IDEAL RESPONSE GUIDANCE (TE ONLY)

Responses should:

- remain analytical, not devotional
- cite historical examples directly
- distinguish faith from institution
- avoid personal testimony

# WRITING TASKS (HS)

## Analytical Essay

**Prompt:**
Analyze how the Black Church functions as both a refuge and a mechanism of miseducation in Chapter 8.

**Explanatory Writing**

**Prompt:**
Explain how institutional religion contributes to cognitive dissonance among the so-called African American people, using Chapter 8 only.

---

# DISCUSSION PROTOCOL (HS)

**Essential Question:**

"Can faith liberate if it is controlled?"

Discussion norms:

- Text-first responses
- Respect belief diversity
- Academic tone only

---

# KNOWLEDGE OF S.E.L.F. ALIGNMENT — CHAPTER 8

| Domain | Text Connection |
|---|---|
| SELF Conscience | Spiritual awareness |
| SELF Governing | Independent thought |
| Social Conscience | Collective truth |
| Aspirations | Liberation through knowledge |

---

# ASSESSMENT RUBRIC — HS CHAPTER 8

| Category | Points |
|---|---|
| Textual Accuracy | 10 |
| Historical Understanding | 10 |
| Vocabulary Precision | 5 |
| Analytical Reasoning | 5 |
| **Total** | **30** |

# THE MISEDUCATION OF THE NEGRO IN THE 21ST CENTURY

## HIGH SCHOOL TEACHER'S EDITION (GRADES 9–12)

### CHAPTER 9 — REVELATION (FOUR HUNDRED YEARS ARE UP)

**Knowledge of S.E.L.F. (Social Empowerment Learning Framework)**
By **Cedric A. Washington**

---

## TEACHER ORIENTATION — CHAPTER 9 (HS)

**Instructional Focus**

Chapter 9 synthesizes the book's arguments into a **culminating revelation** that links **history, religion, politics, culture, and education**. At the high school level, instruction emphasizes **text-based synthesis**, **chronological reasoning**, and **interpretation of revelation as disclosure of truth**, not prediction.

Students are expected to:

- synthesize claims across chapters
- analyze chronology and causation
- evaluate revelation as knowledge disclosure
- distinguish symbolism from documented patterns

---

## CENTRAL CLAIM (TEXT-ANCHORED)

The miseducation of the Negro is sustained through controlled narratives of history, religion, and politics; when suppressed historical truth is revealed, the mind begins to correct and re-correct itself, signaling the end of a four-hundred-year cycle of confusion.

---

# AUTHOR'S PURPOSE (FROM THE TEXT)

The author:

- defines miseducation as poor, wrong, or harmful education
- situates Black history beyond the Middle Passage
- frames revelation as disclosure of original historical truth
- connects global events to collective consciousness
- calls for collective awakening, organization, and rebuilding

# CHAPTER STRUCTURE (TEXT-FAITHFUL)

## SECTION A — DEFINING MIS-EDUCATION

- Merriam-Webster definition
- Controlled narratives
- Confusion of origin

## SECTION B — SEPARATION OF CHURCH AND STATE

- Neutrality and interpretation
- Public use of scripture
- Institutional contradiction

## SECTION C — PRE-SLAVERY HISTORY

- Twelve Tribes of Israel
- Deuteronomy 28
- Scattering and loss of culture

## SECTION D — POLITICS & PARTICIPATION

- Voting patterns
- Party allegiance
- Repeated unmet demands

## SECTION E — FOUR HUNDRED YEARS

- 1619 timeline
- COVID-19 global pause
- Collective disruption

---

## SECTION F — REVELATION DEFINED

- Disclosure of truth
- Recognition of patterns
- Correction of thought

---

## SECTION G — CALL TO ACTION

- Collective organization
- Cultural rebuilding
- Community ownership

---

# VOCABULARY (TEXT-DERIVED — HS)

Students analyze **culminating conceptual language**.

| Term | Meaning from Context |
|---|---|
| miseducation | poor, wrong, harmful education |
| revelation | disclosed truth |
| chronology | sequence of events |
| interpretation | assigned meaning |
| neutrality | institutional avoidance |
| narrative | controlled story |
| diaspora | scattered people |
| cognitive dissonance | conflicting beliefs |
| correction | mental realignment |
| disclosure | making truth known |
| prophecy | foretold outcome |
| origin | beginning |
| awakening | realization |

| Term | Meaning from Context |
|---|---|
| collective | unified people |
| restitution | what is owed |

# TEXT-DEPENDENT QUESTIONS (HS)

## Synthesis & Evaluation

1. How does the author define miseducation, and why is that definition central to the chapter?
2. Why is pre-slavery history essential to revelation?
3. How does separation of church and state contribute to confusion?
4. Why is the four-hundred-year timeline significant?
5. How does the author interpret global disruption as revelation?
6. What does "correct and re-correct the mind" mean in this chapter?
7. What responsibilities accompany revelation?

# IDEAL RESPONSE GUIDANCE (TE ONLY)

Responses should:

- synthesize multiple sections
- use chronological evidence
- avoid speculation
- distinguish belief from analysis

# WRITING TASKS (HS)

## Culminating Analytical Essay

**Prompt:**
Explain how revelation functions as the corrective force to miseducation in Chapter 9, using only text evidence.

**Synthesis Writing**

**Prompt:**
Analyze how history, religion, and politics converge in Chapter 9 to signal the end of miseducation.

---

# DISCUSSION PROTOCOL (HS)

**Essential Question:**

"What happens when suppressed truth is revealed?"

Guidelines:

- Cite specific sections
- Maintain academic tone
- Avoid theological debate

---

# KNOWLEDGE OF S.E.L.F. ALIGNMENT — CHAPTER 9

| Domain | Text Connection |
|---|---|
| SELF Conscience | Historical awareness |
| SELF Governing | Independent thinking |
| Social Conscience | Collective responsibility |
| Aspirations | Rebuilding destiny |

---

# ASSESSMENT RUBRIC — HS CHAPTER 9

| Category | Points |
|---|---|
| Textual Synthesis | 10 |
| Chronological Reasoning | 10 |
| Vocabulary Precision | 5 |
| Interpretive Accuracy | 5 |
| **Total** | **30** |

# APPENDICES

## APPENDIX A

### AUTHOR'S PHILOSOPHY OF EDUCATION (TEXT-DERIVED)

Education is defined in the text as a **systemic process of instruction**, while knowledge is defined as **information and experience that produces intelligence and wisdom**. The author asserts that when education is controlled by an oppressor, it results in **miseducation**—poor, wrong, or harmful instruction that disconnects students from identity, culture, and truth.

Teaching, in this framework, is not compliance to models but **cultural responsibility**. Intelligence is cultivated through **culture**, and behavior is the visible outcome of intelligence shaped by environment. Therefore, authentic education must be culturally grounded, historically accurate, and community-centered.

# APPENDIX B

## GLOSSARY OF TERMS (TEXT-EXCLUSIVE)

**All terms listed below appear directly in the manuscript and are defined strictly by contextual usage.**

| Term | Contextual Meaning |
|---|---|
| Miseducation | Poor, wrong, or harmful education |
| Knowledge | Information and experience that produce intelligence |
| Education | Systematic instruction |
| Intelligence | Ability to acquire and apply knowledge |
| Culture | Attitudes, behaviors, and practices of a people |
| Behavior | Actions produced by intelligence |
| Privilege | Access granted by systems |
| Figurehead | Nominal leader without real power |
| Cognitive Dissonance | Conflicting beliefs causing rejection of truth |
| Revelation | Disclosure of suppressed truth |
| Narrative | Controlled historical story |
| Origin | True beginning of a people |
| Diaspora | Scattering of a nation of people |
| Prophecy | Foretold outcome |
| Liberation | Freedom from mental and systemic bondage |
| Empowerment | Gaining control over identity and destiny |
| Systemic | Embedded within institutions |
| Culture = Intelligence = Behavior | Foundational equation of the text |

# APPENDIX C

## CHRONOLOGICAL FRAMEWORK (TEXT-ALIGNED)

This timeline is used for **instructional reference only** and reflects **authorial sequencing**, not interpretation.

- Pre-Slavery: Twelve Tribes of Israel
- Transatlantic Slave Trade
- 1619 – Arrival in Jamestown, Virginia
- Slavery (246 years)
- Jim Crow (1865–1968)
- Civil Rights Era (1960s)
- Voting Rights Act (1965)
- 1989 – "African American" terminology
- 2008–2016 – First Black President
- 2019–2020 – COVID-19 Global Pause
- 2020 – Global protests
- Present – Revelation Phase

# APPENDIX D

## KNOWLEDGE OF S.E.L.F. ALIGNMENT (HS)

| SELF Mastery | Manuscript Connection |
|---|---|
| SELF Conscience | Identity, origin, awareness |
| SELF Governing | Independent thought |
| Social Conscience | Collective responsibility |
| Aspirations | Rebuilding destiny |
| Good People Skills | Community accountability |

# APPENDIX E

## ELA STANDARDS ALIGNMENT (HS)

### Reading Informational Text

- Analyze central ideas
- Evaluate arguments
- Trace historical reasoning
- Determine meaning of words in context

### Writing

- Text-based analysis
- Argumentative writing
- Synthesis across texts
- Use of evidence

### Speaking & Listening

- Structured discussion
- Evidence-based dialogue
- Academic language

# APPENDIX F

## SOCIAL STUDIES STANDARDS ALIGNMENT (HS)

- Historical analysis
- Chronology and causation
- Civic engagement
- Political systems
- Cultural identity

# APPENDIX G

## ASSESSMENT OVERVIEW (HS)

| Assessment Type | Purpose |
| --- | --- |
| Text-Dependent Questions | Comprehension |
| Analytical Essays | Synthesis |
| Discussion Protocols | Oral reasoning |
| Culminating Project | Application |
| Reflection Writing | Metacognition |

# APPENDIX H

## DISCUSSION NORMS (HS)

- Speak from text evidence
- Respect lived experience
- Avoid theological debate
- Analyze systems, not individuals
- Focus on literacy and reasoning

# APPENDIX I

## CITATION & SOURCE POLICY

All instruction:

- derives from the original manuscript
- uses author-cited sources only
- avoids supplemental interpretations

This Teacher's Edition is a **primary instructional document**, not an anthology.

# APPENDIX J

## DISTRICT / DOE READINESS STATEMENT

This curriculum:

- aligns to ELA and Social Studies standards
- integrates SEL without political advocacy
- centers literacy, history, and analysis
- is appropriate for Grades 9–12

www.ingramcontent.com/pod-product-compliance
Lightning Source LLC
Chambersburg PA
CBHW041611260326
41914CB00012B/1460